D0803459

DOGS SET VIII

BERNESE MOUNTAIN DOGS

Jill C. Wheeler
ABDO Publishing Company

visit us at
www.abdopublishing.com

Published by ABDO Publishing Company, 8000 West 78th Street, Edina, Minnesota 55439. Copyright © 2010 by Abdo Consulting Group, Inc. International copyrights reserved in all countries. No part of this book may be reproduced in any form without written permission from the publisher. The Checkerboard Library™ is a trademark and logo of ABDO Publishing Company.

Printed in the United States of America, North Mankato, Minnesota.
082009
012010

♻ PRINTED ON RECYCLED PAPER

Cover Photo: Alamy
Interior Photos: Alamy pp. 9, 11, 13, 17, 19, 20–21; Corbis p. 5; iStockphoto pp. 7, 15

Series Coordinator: Tamara L. Britton
Editors: Tamara L. Britton, BreAnn Rumsch
Art Direction: Jaime Martens

Library of Congress Cataloging-in-Publication Data

Wheeler, Jill C., 1964-
  Bernese mountain dogs / Jill C. Wheeler.
      p. cm. -- (Dogs)
  Includes index.
  ISBN 978-1-60453-781-9
  1. Bernese mountain dog--Juvenile literature. I. Title.
  SF429.B47W44 2010
  636.73--dc22
                                2009027726

CONTENTS

The Dog Family 4

Bernese Mountain Dogs 6

What They're Like 8

Coat and Color 10

Size 12

Care 14

Feeding 16

Things They Need 18

Puppies 20

Glossary 22

Web Sites 23

Index 24

THE DOG FAMILY

Dogs are popular pets. There are about 400 million dogs worldwide! All these dogs belong to the family **Canidae**. The name comes from the Latin word *canis*, which means "dog." This family also includes wolves, coyotes, and foxes.

For many years, dogs and humans have been close companions. At first, dogs helped people hunt. Over time, people began **breeding** dogs to help with other activities. Today, there are nearly 400 dog breeds.

Dogs have had many important jobs since they were **domesticated**. Bernese mountain dogs were bred as working dogs. They were meant to herd livestock and haul heavy loads.

Bernese
mountain dogs

BERNESE MOUNTAIN DOGS

No one knows exactly when the Bernese mountain dog **breed** began. However about 2,000 years ago, Roman warriors invaded Switzerland. Many people believe they brought ancestors of Bernese mountain dogs with them.

Bernese mountain dogs are named for the Swiss state of Bern. The Bernese Alps are in this area. These hard-working, loyal dogs are called Berners for short.

Berners were important members of Swiss farm families. They helped drive cattle, pull carts, and guard livestock. They also guarded the farms and made good family companions.

The Bernese mountain dog came to the United States in 1926. In 1937, the **American Kennel Club (AKC)** recognized the **breed**. Today, the Berner is the AKC's fortieth most popular breed.

In Switzerland, this strong, intelligent breed is called the Berner Sennenhund.

WHAT THEY'RE LIKE

Bernese mountain dogs are big! Many owners would say their dogs have big hearts, too. These gentle giants are self-confident, calm, affectionate, and smart.

Berners are also good-natured animals. They do well with children. And they get along with other pets, including dogs.

Although Berners are natural watchdogs, they are not problem barkers. They are not **aggressive** unless threatened. They can even appear shy around strangers.

The Bernese mountain dog has a steady, happy-go-lucky attitude. This is one dog that loves

8

companionship. So it needs to live inside with its family, not outside in a pen. Life is good for a Berner when it joins in family activities!

Berners bond quickly with their families and make loving companions.

COAT AND COLOR

Bernese mountain dogs are often noticed for their striking, tricolor coats. The medium-length hair can be straight or slightly wavy. It is jet-black and accented with white and rust-colored markings.

The rust color appears over each eye, on the cheeks, and under the tail. It also highlights the sides of the chest and all four legs. There is white fur on the **muzzle** and forehead. Additional white markings color the tip of the Berner's tail and feet. The dog also sports a bold, white chest.

Bernese mountain dogs are double coated. They have a thick undercoat below a longer top coat. This makes their coats weather resistant. It also makes them easy to keep clean, as their coats easily shed dirt.

However, this thick coat means extra work in hot weather! Berners can shed heavily. Frequent brushing will help keep the coat in good shape. This is especially important during the heavy shedding season.

The Berner's coat is called tricolor *because it contains three colors.*

SIZE

Bernese mountain dogs are sturdy, well-built animals. Adult males usually stand 25 to 27 inches (63 to 68 cm) tall at the shoulder. They can weigh 80 to 115 pounds (36 to 52 kg). Adult females often weigh 70 to 95 pounds (31 to 43 kg). They stand 23 to 26 inches (58 to 66 cm) tall.

The Berner is slightly longer than it is tall. As a working dog, it must be able to handle heavy loads. Its strong, muscular body helps it pull lots of weight.

The Berner has a broad, flat-topped head. Its ears are triangular with rounded tips. The Berner has a strong, straight **muzzle** with a black nose. It has dark brown, oval-shaped eyes.

Though large and heavy, the Berner is quick and graceful.

When it is alert, the Berner carries its bushy
tail with an upward curl. It carries its tail low
when it is resting. The Berner's normal stride is a
slow trot. But when necessary, it can run fast!

CARE

Like all dogs, Bernese mountain dogs need physical and mental exercise. They need at least 30 minutes of moderate exercise daily.

However, it is important not to overwork a Berner. The Berner is naturally suited for cold weather. In hot weather, its thick coat and large size can cause overheating. This can make a Berner very ill. So, owners should keep their Berners cool on hot days.

As with other dogs, it is necessary to groom a Berner. It is a good idea to check its skin, nose, mouth, eyes, and feet each week. A Berner's teeth should be brushed daily. And, its nails should be trimmed regularly.

Berners are subject to health problems such as **cancer**, joint problems, and **bloat**. A veterinarian can help keep a Berner healthy. The veterinarian can also provide **vaccines**. He or she can **spay** or **neuter** the Berner, too.

FEEDING

Not every dog needs the same amount of food. Puppies may require three to four small meals a day. Older, less active dogs may need only one meal a day.

Each Bernese mountain dog's food requirements depend on several factors. These include the dog's age, size, and rate of exercise. A veterinarian can suggest a diet based on each dog's needs.

Berners need a regular meal schedule, with an occasional treat. This will maintain proper weight and health. Two or three small meals a day instead of one large meal will reduce the chance of **bloat**. And all dogs need plenty of clean, fresh water.

Eating a good-quality food will help a Berner stay healthy.

THINGS THEY NEED

Because of their large size, Bernese mountain dogs need plenty of space. This is not a good **breed** for someone who lives in an apartment or a small house. A Berner can clear a coffee table with a wag of its tail!

Berners need room to run and play. They are happiest with a large living area and a fenced yard. Every Berner requires a collar on which to hang license and identification tags. Large, sturdy food and water dishes are a must.

More important than things from the store are a loving family, **socialization**, and training. Early obedience training and socialization will result in good behavior.

Companionship is very important to Berners. Berners can be very unhappy when they are alone for long periods of time.

A Berner will also need a warm, soft bed.

PUPPIES

Bernese mountain dogs are **pregnant** for about 63 days. They give birth to an average of eight puppies in a **litter**.

Berner puppies need to stay with their mother until they are 8 to 12 weeks old. Then, they can move with their family to their forever home.

If you have decided that a Berner is right for your family, look for a reputable **breeder**. When choosing a puppy, look for playful and curious Berners. They should be willing to approach people and be held.

When your puppy comes home, feed it the same diet it ate at the breeder's. At first, Berner puppies may need a special diet to manage their growth rate. Growing too fast can damage their young bones.

It is best to **socialize** your puppy early. Expose your Berner to different experiences, animals, and people. This will help it grow into a well-adjusted dog. A healthy, well cared for Berner will be a loving member of your family for six to nine years.

Puppies are born blind and deaf. They can see and hear after about two weeks. At three weeks, they take their first steps.

GLOSSARY

aggressive - displaying hostility.

American Kennel Club (AKC) - an organization that studies and promotes interest in purebred dogs.

bloat - a condition in which food and gas trapped in a dog's stomach cause pain, shock, and even death.

breed - a group of animals sharing the same ancestors and appearance. A breeder is a person who raises animals. Raising animals is often called breeding them.

cancer - any of a group of often deadly diseases marked by harmful changes in the normal growth of cells. Cancer can spread and destroy healthy tissues and organs.

Canidae (KAN-uh-dee) - the scientific Latin name for the dog family. Members of this family are called canids. They include domestic dogs, wolves, jackals, foxes, and coyotes.

domesticated - adapted to life with humans.

litter - all of the puppies born at one time to a mother dog.

22

muzzle - an animal's nose and jaws.

neuter (NOO-tuhr) - to remove a male animal's reproductive organs.

pregnant - having one or more babies growing within the body.

socialize - to accustom an animal or a person to spending time with others.

spay - to remove a female animal's reproductive organs.

vaccine (vak-SEEN) - a shot given to animals or humans to prevent them from getting an illness or a disease.

WEB SITES

To learn more about Bernese mountain dogs, visit ABDO Publishing Company on the World Wide Web at **www.abdopublishing.com**. Web sites about Bernese mountain dogs are featured on our Book Links page. These links are routinely monitored and updated to provide the most current information available.

INDEX

A
American Kennel
    Club 7

B
body 10, 12, 14
breeder 20

C
Canidae (family) 4
character 6, 8, 9,
    18, 19, 20, 21
chest 10
coat 10, 11, 14
collar 18
color 10, 12

E
ears 12
exercise 14, 16
eyes 10, 12, 14

F
feet 10, 14
food 16, 18, 20

G
grooming 11, 14

H
head 10, 12
health 14, 15, 16,
    21
history 4, 6, 7

L
legs 10
license 18
life span 21

M
mouth 14
muzzle 10, 12

N
nails 14
neuter 15
nose 12, 14

P
puppies 16, 20, 21

R
reproduction 20

S
shedding 10, 11
size 8, 12, 14, 16,
    18
spay 15
Switzerland 6

T
tail 10, 13, 18
teeth 14
training 18, 21

U
United States 7

V
vaccines 15
veterinarian 15, 16

W
water 16, 18
work 4, 6, 8, 12